# Monaco

Watch out for the shooting black ichor
It would be good if you were to come from the sky
The sky's honeysuckle is climbing
The earthly octopi are throbbing
And so very many of us have become our own gravediggers
Pale octopi of the chalky waves O octopi with pale beaks
Around the house is this ocean that you know well
       And is never still

- Apollinaire

**From:** sergeant-rock@gmail.com
**To:** robinsonrj191@gmail.com
**Date:** 19 April 2022, 23:43
**Subject:** Hello from Monte-Carlo

Darling,

Nightmare journey to Nice this morning ... train delayed to Gatwick (as always, it doesn't matter who runs that franchise), then two hours late because of staff shortages. Maybe they all had Covid, or maybe the pandemic finally made all this cheap air travel unsustainable, as we always knew would happen at some point. It feels weird to be going abroad again. It'll be the first time since that weekend at the Biennale in September 2019, just after The World Transformed and JC's speech on the Old Steine when you took my arm and said *we're going to win*, then we spoke all the way to Venice about how we didn't need to live in times that were any more interesting. My heart still breaks but we don't need to go over that December and everything after, all those doors slammed in our faces. My friends tell me not to keep dwelling on it and I know they're right. Honestly, it's nice just to be out of the house, I had a ludicrous row with Soph last week that began with her getting stroppy with me for leaving my bike in the hallway (which I've done ever since I moved in FFS) and ended up with her accusing me of making too much noise in the mornings, not doing the washing-up, the usual house-sharing stuff that became a nightmare during lockdown, I'm way too old for it.

My therapist told me to take a break, maybe somewhere I hadn't been before, somewhere I wouldn't normally go.

Mum thought so too. (She's still up and down, by the way – I keep telling her she needs to get over dad, try to meet new people. She still won't go anywhere with anyone she doesn't know in case she gets Covid, but who am I to talk about new people?) They both know I'm skint (and I'm starting to wonder if it'll be better for my mental health to just save that £50 a week) and I got quite annoyed with them for suggesting it. Two days later, though, Chris at *Photo World* got in touch, and we agreed that I could go and "capture Monaco" and the "atmosphere" of the place in the run-up to the Grand Prix. Last year's had a limited audience and the 2020 one was cancelled, so it'll be the first 'normal' one since 2019. I'd have to sort out travel and accommodation myself, but I could expense them, so why the fuck not? I wanted to come for the actual race – but it's impossible to find a place to stay then without spending crazy money, so Chris suggested I come and see what Monaco is like when they're getting ready for it. My therapist said I should fork out for a nice place, but I can't afford that, so it's easyJet and Airbnb, staying in a flat on the French border (near a town called Beausoleil) in what's very obviously a child's bedroom – *Asterix* comics, map on the wall, the works. I'm sleeping in a bunk bed – haven't done that since I was about six! So close to the ceiling I'm worried I'll bang my head when I get up tomorrow …

I got a taste of how expensive it'd be just coming from the airport. The bus – not a taxi, a *bus* – from Nice was €22 for a half-hour journey! Everyone's still wearing masks here btw. (Remember when it was just the Chinese students at the art schools, and it all seemed so foreboding?) They had to give me one of those itchy surgical ones for the plane because they didn't like the black one I got from Boots. Anyway, I got here around 6pm, Jean-Philippe, the host, sent his kid to greet me in the foyer and you'll be amused to hear my French is still at GCSE level, *bonjour, ou est ma chambre*, not much else. Remember that day in Sète, when *every single person* replied to me in English? (And you joked about how I pronounced 'Paul Valéry' "as in Valerie Solanas" – something no-one else in the world would've said.)

Anyway, I walked back down the hill to the plaza where the bus dropped me off, and I have to admit it's beautiful. Palm trees around a little square, those twirling paper flowers (what are they called?), ferns and flowers, a bust of some Prince near a fountain between the square and the casino with its turrets and its big domed roof. It's so strange walking in a city without you, I keep expecting you to point out a statue of some long-forgotten politician or an Art Nouveau façade or some funny public art and now I'm just keeping my eyes peeled and doing some Googling. It's not the same. I walked through the Jardin Japonais on my way to Plage du Larvotto and wanted to send you photos of every plant and their descriptions, to show you how weirdly perfect it all is, and to laugh at all the uptight women in their Chanel suits with their fluffy little handbag dogs. Somehow, they make a bit more sense here than on the tube, but that's just the type of place it is …

Until soon xxx

*Jardins de la Petite Afrique*

**From:** sergeant-rock@gmail.com
**To:** robinsonrj191@gmail.com
**Date:** 21 April 2022, 01:21
**Subject:** Re: Hello from Monte-Carlo

Darling,

I walked all day, and now I'm exhausted. I can feel my heartbeat as I lie on the bunk bed. Maybe it's anxiety, maybe cholesterol, I don't know. It's not a relapse, though. I had another scan two weeks ago and got the all-clear. It felt so wrong, not even texting you – the first person I WhatsApped was mum, who just replied 'good'. I've thought about telling you ever since, I hope you don't mind.

**From:** sergeant-rock@gmail.com
**To:** robinsonrj191@gmail.com
**Date:** 21 April 2022, 09:33
**Subject:** (no subject)

I woke up early and put my hand out to reach for you, like I still do every morning, but there wasn't even another pillow. I showered, dressed, left without speaking to anyone, bought a croissant and a little carton of apple juice from the local Carrefour (doing the entire transaction in French, you would've laughed). I walked back down past the casino, taking pictures of the scaffolding for the temporary stands for the Grand Prix. The Fairmont Hairpin is just around the corner, with a sign calling it 'the world's most famous bend', apparently named after the hotel there that charges a fortune when the race is on. (I thought it'd be the other way round). I could see the road markings for the race, and on the side of one of the stands, a list of previous winners, going all the way back to 1929. But that's all there was really, just a few examples of how the Grand Prix is woven into the place – the museum for Prince Rainier's car collection, a trophy from 1950 in a window and a statue of Fangio (who, according to the list, only won it twice – I think it's more because he won so many championships). There were a couple of big Formula 1 stores and F1 tat in every tourist trap, so people are really into it, way more than the Masters tennis tournament, which was last week, or the football. (I'm sure you know this, but the local team play in the French league, and apparently they're pretty good at the moment. I saw the police with a load of fans earlier, shouting and letting off flares, Jean-Philippe said they were from Nice and that they absolutely *hate* Monaco ...)

There wasn't much to cover about the GP unless I started talking to people who were actually involved with it, which isn't easy. I'd forgotten how much I hate covering any kind of sport because it's always so hard to get interviews with anyone (and even when you do, they never have much to say). I realised I didn't even know who I wanted to meet. Drivers? Mechanics? Fans? There's no way I'd be allowed anywhere near the racers, let alone the owners, and what would fans say other than "I'm looking forward to the Grand Prix"? It seems pretty obvious now, but I just didn't think of it when Chris and I were emailing, all I wanted was to get out of London for a bit and so I didn't really notice how little thought he seemed to be putting into it.

I couldn't help remembering that time we watched *Senna*. I kept it to myself at the time as I didn't want another argument, but I wasn't that interested, it was your choice. I don't think I'd be here now if I hadn't seen it, because it was incredible, such a simple story so perfectly told, Senna the young and beautiful outsider up against the fusty old Prost and the establishment, determined to have F1 made safer while driving like a maniac, and eventually killed in a crash that looked fairly innocuous when he didn't want to race because someone else had died the day before, and an entire nation going into mourning. Here, of course, I couldn't stop thinking about it, seeing that mural with Senna as champion five times in a row – why isn't there a statue of him here?

I've decided to expand outwards – to capture Monaco more generally, through its buildings and sculptures more than its people. Honestly, this place is tiny – the smallest country in the world (the Vatican doesn't count), and not even as big as Horsham. I saw most of it last night and today. The harbour is gorgeous at night, and there are lots of modern buildings, but they haven't just dumped Dubai onto Port Hercule like with the Thames. No skyscrapers, just low-rise concrete blocks climbing up the hills. I walked along the beach, past this 'Promenade du Champions' where lots of footballers had left their footprints (I didn't recognise the names but I'm sure you would've), through the Japanese garden I told you about, on to the Grimaldi Forum, which is like the glass base of a pyramid, and the artificial beach at Larvotto. That just about sums this place up: expensively imported sand on reclaimed land and a single palm tree. I was surprised it wasn't private, but then again I didn't see any riff-raff for them to keep out – that was obviously decided centuries ago, and apparently their working class live around Beausoleil. But it's already past one, and you'll have gone to bed. I'll climb back into my bunk, trying not to wake the kids in the bedroom next door, in the same way I've had to tiptoe around Soph back home lately … Hopefully she'll calm down a bit while I'm away. Tomorrow I'm going to the Prince's Palace xxx

*The harbour at night*

*Fairmont Hairpin*

**From:** sergeant-rock@gmail.com
**To:** robinsonrj191@gmail.com
**Date:** 21 April 2022, 23:18
**Subject:** La Solitude

Darling,

I didn't do any research on Monaco before I came here. It's so small and I figured anyone interesting would've gone to France and ... that's true, but I still found some traces of fascinating people who grew up here, as well as a few who moved here because they were tax exiles, gamblers, hedonists, fraudsters or whatever. (There's an Erich von Stroheim film about this called *Foolish Wives*, but they recreated the whole of Monte-Carlo in Hollywood, focusing on the casino, I'll watch it when I get home ...)

This bust caught my eye when I first got here, and as soon as I saw 'musicien-poete', I wanted to know who he was. I found a *Best of Léo Ferré* on YouTube and loved it. I was expecting something like Serge Gainsbourg, just because Ferré's also a French (or *Monégasque*, as they call people from here) singer from the 60s. It's strangely light yet intense at same time, he flits between tightly controlled piano playing or menacing talking and absolutely hammering the keys and shouting over an operatic backing chorus. I relate to him a lot, I wish I had an outlet like that where I could just let go and not have to put up with bullshit from my housemates, fake-left fuckboys on Hinge, all the Tories and Lib Dems I meet through work ... The compilation had a lot of live tracks and his audience just go wild at the end of every *chanson*. I put it on my phone and listened to him all day as I walked around, it felt like an appropriate soundtrack. (Maybe it'll help with my French, just a little bit …)

I'm doing the same kind of exploring as when we went away together, galleries and museums, looking out for statues and monuments, public art and graffiti. Monaco's far weirder than I expected, though. I never imagined I'd come here, and I can't believe I'm saying it, but *I think I like it* – or at least I don't hate it. There are stupid boards everywhere saying shit like 'Monaco – Land of Ahead Thinkers' and obviously the yacht club can fuck off, but some of it is kind of funny: I saw this ludicrous poster with Mickey and Minnie Mouse, the Monopoly Man, Bugs Bunny and Jessica Rabbit playing poker by the casino, I couldn't tell if it was shit art or just an annoying advert. Of course, the most straightforward adverts for Gucci or superyacht insurance or banks give a better measure of who lives and works here, but I haven't met anyone besides Jean-Philippe, and I've only said a few words to him, so I've just been walking around with the camera.

I thought it'd be interesting to see the Prince's Palace (I'd never dream of doing the same in London) but it was closed for refurbishment, so I went to the churches in the old town. I had to queue up to see Princess Grace's grave in St Nicholas Cathedral, obviously all the tourists want to see that. (I was more taken by *Le Christ mort* by a sculptor called François Bosio – I've sent you a picture, Bosio is as big a deal as Ferré here, I think.) Her grave is simple and dignified, and that's something I noticed: when I end up around rich people in London, usually through the art world, they're so fucking *gauche*, tacky *nouveau riche* bastards, here at least things are more tasteful and there's some faded *fin-de-siècle* glamour. Maybe it's just me but there's a melancholy running through the Principality, partly because Rainier III turned it into a big shrine to Grace Kelly: there's a rose garden and theatre named after her, several statues, and this *Parcours Princesse Grace* of their marriage, her meeting the *Ballets Russes*, helping sick little children, etc. Maybe that's why there's no monument to Senna: they were all mourning the Princess. (I don't know how organic that is. I guess it's led from the top rather than being like those people flocking to Kensington Palace after Diana died, not least as there are so few *Monégasques*, but the whole Grace Kelly funeral is on YouTube if you want to judge for yourself.)

*Bust of Léo Ferré*

*Princess Grace's grave*

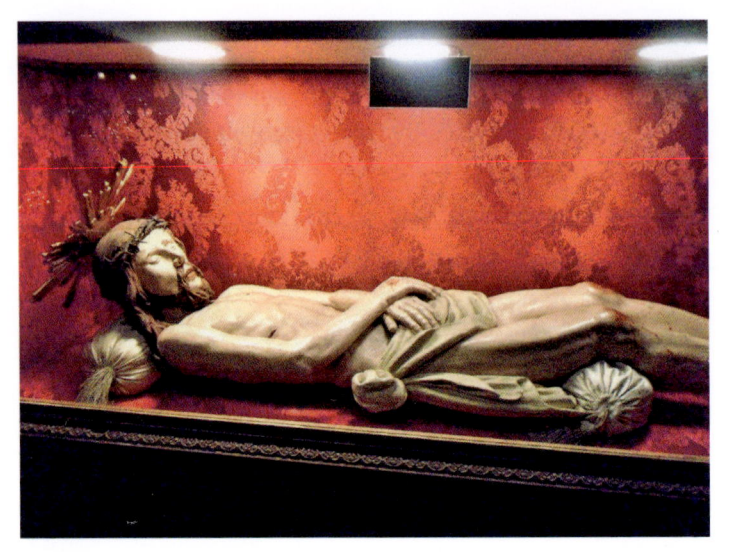

*François Bosio – Le Christ mort*

**From:** sergeant-rock@gmail.com
**To:** robinsonrj191@gmail.com
**Date:** 22 April 2022, 03:31
**Subject:** Ne chantez pas la mort

Thinking about death ("as usual" you'd say), I went to the cemetery. Monaco was neutral but there was still a big World War I memorial, I think some nationals signed up for France – apparently there was a big succession crisis in 1918 because the French objected to the possibility of a German national taking the throne, and now the French get to approve whoever takes over. (There was a revolution in 1910 as well, but sadly they got a constitutional monarchy rather than a republic and well, we know what kind of country *that* gives you, don't we? That said, I keep seeing newsstands with stuff about the French election with Macron and Le Pen, and I'm not sure I'd swap Johnson and fucking Starmer for them ...) Monaco was neutral in World War II as well but got occupied by the Italians and the Germans, and there's another memorial (from 2015) for the 90 Jews who were sent to the camps. Otherwise, there were some incredibly grand tombs – mausolea, really – for Barons and a few other rich people, and an interesting one for an architect called Théodore Gastaud (who was one of the revolutionaries). I found Léo Ferré's – again, very simple – and my favourite, Josephine Baker. Princess Grace gave Josephine a villa after she got evicted from her French *château* with her 12 children and arranged a big comeback concert for her in Monte-Carlo. (I watched some old footage online of her singing *It's Impossible* which you'd love.)

I suggested to Chris that I make my piece about Monaco's public art rather than F1. They have so much of it – they can afford it, after all. I don't like it all, but the whole place feels like an outdoor gallery. (I know what you're thinking: "A bit like Harlow …") Some of it's just embedded into everyday life – there's a Ben (Vautier) text saying 'Life is too short to drink bad wine' outside a bar, which you'd just walk past if you didn't recognise his handwriting. But lots of stuff jumps out at you: an Anish Kapoor 'sky mirror' outside the casino, which is better than that shit helter skelter he did for the Olympics, and a few things that feel a bit kitsch, but there are good things in the sculpture gardens, around the harbour and in town. Some of our favourite artists, too – Giorgio De Chirico, Fernando Botero (in that weird Promenade du Champions I told you about) – and plenty I don't know, someone called Emma de Sigaldi crops up a lot, and Kees Verkade, who did something outside the football stadium and a statue of Prince Rainier. Who knows – might even be a book in it? I've sent you a few of them, anyway, but there's so much more here that I want to share with you … Starting to feel, I don't know, *comfortable* here? xxx

*Grave of Josephine Baker*

*Ben – 'Life is too short to drink bad wine'*

*Anish Kapoor – Sky Mirror (1999)*

*Anna Chromý – Ulysses (2000)*

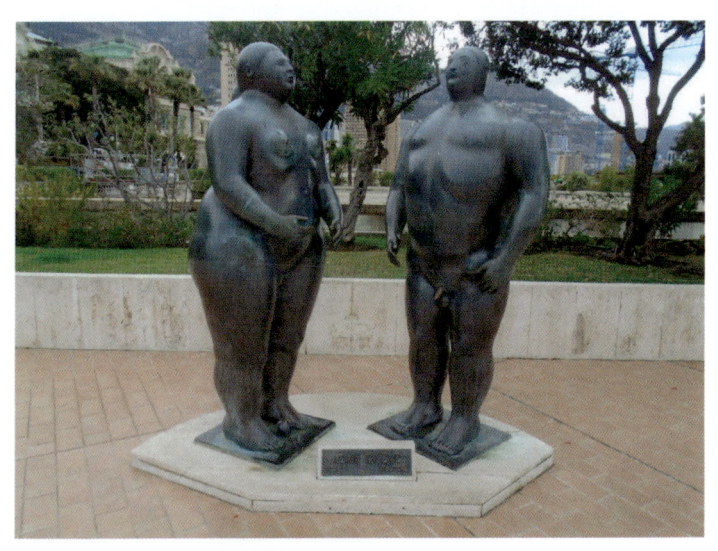

*Fernando Botero – Adam et Eve (1981)*

**From:** sergeant-rock@gmail.com
**To:** robinsonrj191@gmail.com
**Date:** 22 April 2022, 06:38
**Subject:** Songs of the Poorly Loved

I haven't heard from you for so long, but you're in my thoughts so much. *Everything* reminds me of you. In the old town last night, this plaque caught my eye.

And it reminded me of one of my favourite poems of his. I read almost every poem in *Alcools* to you, in English and in my faltering French, but I never shared this one because I knew that the moment I did, that would be the end. But I know it off by heart, in English anyway:

> *I picked this sprig of heather*
> *Autumn has died you must remember*
> *We shall not see each other ever*
> *I'm waiting and you must remember*
> *Time's perfume is a sprig of heather*

I'm going to try to go back to sleep.

If this *Farewell* moves you – write.

*Plaque for Guillaume Apollinaire*
*Donald Revell's translation of Apollinaire's 'The Farewell' in Alcools*
*Published by Wesleyan University Press in 1995*

**From:** sergeant-rock@gmail.com
**To:** robinsonrj191@gmail.com
**Date:** 23 April 2022, 00:04
**Subject:** (no subject)

Still nothing from you, I understand if you're busy or whatever but I hope you don't feel like you can't let me know, or just say hi. Speaking of which, Chris wrote back saying Monaco's public art was "boring". I don't know why I asked tbh: what else was he going to say? Instead, he asked me to focus on the "glamour of the place". (Maybe I should send him the Mickey Mouse casino picture?) He said he knew this was "off-brand" for me, but then it's "off-brand" for me to be in Monaco, and maybe that would make the piece more interesting?

I was in the NMNM – the National Museum – when he emailed. Apparently they used to have this amazing display of dolls and automata, that wasn't on but there was a nice exhibition about Surrealism in Egypt and Monaco. I can see why Surrealists came here, not just because of their fascination with Apollinaire but because the place is so strange. It might not have had all that sculpture or Princess Grace ephemera back then but that mixture of an *ancien régime* that pins its survival to the gambling industry, and an aristocracy that's an endless target for swindlers is *so* compelling. Obviously there was no communist movement here (although it does feel like there's socialism for the rich, with free lifts up the hills, how clean everything is, etc.), but there was an anarchist group, hiding from the Italian government. That sounds like something from an André Gide novel, but the Surrealists detested Gide. (Did I ever show you Benjamin Péret's poem about Gide's conversion to Communism? Y*es you'll have communism monsieur comrade Gide / Sickle in your guts / Hammer down your throat* ...) Léo Ferré was an anarchist too, and I understand why, growing up here meant he wasn't stupid enough to think the rich would ever allow people to vote away their wealth, as we should've known in London ...

Anyway, I learned about Leonor Fini coming here in June 1940 when Monaco was neutral, and falling in love with an Italian consul who became an artist, Stanislao Lepri. So they stayed until 1943, when the Fascists invaded Monaco and set up a puppet state, then Mussolini was ousted and arrested (before the partisans turned him upside down), and the Nazis came, so they went to Italy. The work here wasn't from that time, but Lepri wouldn't have taken up art without it, and I liked his paintings even if they ripped off Fini. (She got credit for her style, rather than it going to him – a nice change.)

Chris's email meant time was tight so I raced around the rest of it – I liked Cléa Badaro and Abdul Kader El Janabi, especially his collages of film stars like Ava Gardner – and then went looking for "glamour". (Remember how we always went out of our way to avoid it when we were out in town? And how we were never sure if our complaints about "bourgeois decadence" were genuinely felt, a bitter parody of middle-class leftists, or – let's be honest – a stab at ourselves?) I went to the Musée Oceanographique and then the Jardin Exotique, only to find it closed for repairs. They'd opened a temporary garden in a big greenhouse but it wasn't the same, there was hardly anyone there and something about that closed space made me feel even less comfortable about asking who they were, let alone if I could pap them.

There weren't many people milling around the Roseraie Princesse Grace either, so I walked back to the flat, wondering what I'd tell Chris. Maybe I'll have to sack it off entirely. In any case, I'm not sure how many people I want to know that I came to Monaco, given that the few I told before I left asked "Why the hell do you want to go there", even if I explain that it was for work and the place is more interesting than they might expect. (I came off all social media – Facebook, Instagram, Twitter – so it won't go on there.) It just struck me that photographing and talking to *workers* would have been a better idea, the men in construction and women in hospitality, perhaps that would cure any romanticism about the place and its "glamour", although doubtless you'd tell me that was just patronising. *Maybe I should find a job here*, I thought as I went past the casino, *no more knocking on doors in the freezing cold and pouring rain, no more "mutual aid" groups where people just take what they want* …

I didn't bring many clothes – I didn't think I'd do much besides walking around – but there was a beautiful dress in one of the boutiques on the Avenue Saint-Michel and I thought *why not*. I'd kept seeing it: red and white with a diagonal sash, I asked to try it on and it fit perfectly. I won't tell you how much it was but more than I've spent on anything else, even that dress I got for Jacqueline's wedding. (How is she, btw? I miss her and Will). It looked absolutely stunning, and the woman just said, "You will wear this a lot." (I showed it to Jean-Philippe and he just smiled and said it looked like the Monaco football shirt.) It was so liberating – letting myself buy something I really wanted – even if it tanked the money I'll get for being here. I went to my room and hung it on the end of the bunk bed. Maybe I'll wear it tomorrow.

*Roseraie Princesse Grace*

*Industrial Monte-Carlo*

**From:** sergeant-rock@gmail.com
**To:** robinsonrj191@gmail.com
**Date:** 23 April 2022, 07:49
**Subject:** Mum

Woken up by a text from mum saying she's got Covid. Called her up, she said she's very tired but basically OK. Perhaps she'll stop worrying and let herself go a bit, I'll chat to her when I'm back. If you don't want me to tell you any of this, let me know x

**From:** sergeant-rock@gmail.com
**To:** robinsonrj191@gmail.com
**Date:** 24 April 2022, 18:25
**Subject:** Les amants tristes

I woke up yesterday morning and thought about taking the camera to Beausoleil – maybe I could get some pictures like the ones of Hackney in lockdown that Chris liked so much. But I could already hear him in the editorial meeting saying "No-one'll be interested in that", so I decided to stick with his advice and go hunting for "glamour". I went back up to the medieval Old Town (*Le Rocher*) and got a *Monegasque* lunch at U Cavagnetu (peppers in olive oil, eggplant in breadcrumbs, octopus), hoping to watch the locals at play. Of course, they were all tourists, and I still had nothing for the assignment. Ha. I went home, stopping to watch people play pétanque and to grab a coffee at the *Place d'Armes* market (where the workers go to eat, apparently), then had a nap.

About 7pm, I got ready to go out. I put on my favourite bra (you know the one), black tights and heels, with the dress I bought here. I hadn't dressed up like that since before the pandemic (I never did for Zoom calls, unlike some people I know), even before the election, I can hardly remember when. I felt so beautiful, and thought that if I threw myself into the world, *something* might happen, even if I didn't know what. I put on my make-up, trying not to go "OTT", smoky eyes and a little lip gloss, to be as classy as the other women here even if I couldn't afford to have a chihuahua in a Hermès handbag.

I'd booked a table in one of the restaurants in the Hôtel de Paris, by the Casino. The plaza was rammed: people were drinking and smoking outside the Café, hanging out by the fountain and looking at that big Anish Kapoor mirror, Bentleys and Rolls Royces dropping off guests in all their finery. (I'm sure *this* was what Chris wanted me to photograph, but there were loads of paparazzi there already, and who's interested in that beyond the fashion rags?) The Hôtel had that faded *fin-de-siècle* romance I told you about, built in the 1860s. You can really imagine Baudelaire, Huysmans and Mirbeau being fascinated by it, with its gold-plated domes and balconies, at least they were in the old drawings, and of course Apollinaire and his mother eating there, in their only set of fine clothes, conning someone else into paying. You'd have puked if you'd seen the inside, I felt overwhelmed by the opulence for the first time, the grand dining room had all these golden arches (I know, "like McDonald's"), chandeliers everywhere, frescos that made me think of Louis Napoléon (and his *Eighteenth Brumaire*) and various others who got what they theirs in 1792.

However it felt to pretend this was my life, I couldn't afford the Michelin-starred ones — two courses for £300! — so I went to La Salle Empire. The waiter could instantly tell I was English and asked if anyone would be joining me. I told him probably not and he handed me the menu without another word. People glanced over but nobody wanted to talk to me — that same snootiness I always felt at home in Surrey, no-one will give you a second unless they've been introduced to you at least twice. I ordered the raw and cooked vegetables as a starter (no photos, I still hate people who post their meals on Insta or wherever), and the roasted lamb for a main. It was expensive, but like those places in London where you get a tiny cut of meat and an asparagus shoot for £50, not a "once in a lifetime" dining experience. Maybe I should have broken the bank and gone to the Louis XV place instead ...

I put on my cardigan – from H&M, it sat awkwardly over my dress – and went to the casino. There were a few people in the foyer but it didn't seem busy, not yet anyway. The guy at the desk wanted to see my passport – citizens of Monaco are banned, apparently because the Prince who licensed it didn't want the locals to piss their money away. He looked me up and down, said "Anglais" with a smile, then asked for €17. For that, I could have either a free drink or a tenner's worth of tokens, so I took the latter. I bought a glass of wine at the bar and sat down, trying to look cool and detached as I clocked the room—who seemed comfortable and who was posing, who was rich (and whether they'd inherited or made their money) and who was pretending, who might actually be *good* at gambling and who was just addicted to it. Chris probably hoped I'd find "glamour" *here*, but photography isn't allowed. (You'll have to imagine it, Google it, or watch one of the hundreds of films that use it as a setting – it's impressive in the same way as the Hôtel, high ceilings and lots of gold, but way bigger).

I attracted as little attention at the bar as in the restaurant – perhaps for the best – so I finished my wine and went into the casino. There were two main rooms, one with fruit machines and roulettes, another with tables for poker and so on. I like card games about as much as you, so I stuck with the first room, starting with the fruit machines. I won my money back at least but it was kind of boring, and I thought I should try something more ambitious.

It was getting busier now, bustling with men in black tie and women in cocktail dresses. Some were hanging out at the bar or having dinner at *Le Train Bleu* (in a train carriage in the Casino). A few were heading for the poker tables, and others were loitering by the roulette. There was a young man in a red shirt and black waistcoat, and an older woman who didn't seem to be playing but stayed at the table. I watched as a few people came and went, brief plays that didn't hit the jackpot, and it stayed empty for a moment, so I thought … *let's try it*.

I tried not to stare at the woman, but I couldn't help thinking of that Apollinaire poem, the one you always used to quote back to me – *That woman was so beautiful / She scared me*. Her face was the colour of Monaco, white skin and red, red lips. A golden headband and earrings, curly hair and a low-cut dress: I was so drawn to her, and then I remembered how Apollinaire's mother worked here as an *entraîneuse*, tempting people into gambling. I wondered if she was doing the same and if that was even allowed any more. I caught her eye and she beckoned me, so maybe, yes.

"You want to play?" asked the man. The pretty redhead smiled at me, and I sat next to her. I tried not to seem too nervous – I'm sure they can sense that here, although I guess it's more of an issue if you're playing poker or something – so I told myself to calm down. I looked her in the eyes and she put a velvet-gloved hand on my knee. "You are going to be *lucky*," she insisted in an accent I couldn't place: Russian, Polish, Italian, I had no idea. I just laughed.

The man asked if I knew how it worked. I said I could bet on a single number, or across red or black, and the woman laughed too. I only had €10, which wasn't enough to go across red or black, or on odd/even or high/low numbers, so I put it all on 24. There were a few people watching, I felt like I was in a film as he spun the wheel, and as the ball bounced around, the woman squeezed my hand. It landed on ... 25. Gasps went up as the man said, "So close, *mademoiselle!*" and raked my chips back into the House. "Would you like to play again?"

Everyone was looking at me, and I suddenly felt how straight and yet *strange* this place was, all these people living out some idea of decadent luxury that they'd learned from a hundred years of cinema. How could I not be the star?

I rushed to the counter and bought €100 of chips. The woman had saved my seat: when I returned, she stroked my back and said, "Be *bold*, darling." I was going to put €5 on 17 (Black), but she told me to be bolder, so I raised it to €10 on 30 (Red). He spun the wheel again: it felt like an eternity but came back on 23, just to one side, so I'd lost another tenner. I wanted to bet on red or black: they said the minimum for that was €20. I sat there, looking at my chips and thinking about my bank balance. "Where are you from?" asked the croupier. I told him, London. "Go on, darling," said a man in a shit Cockney accent, "what've you got to lose?" "20 Euros," I answered plainly, and the people around me laughed. "Will you ever come back to Monte-Carlo?" asked the woman. I hesitated: she smiled at me and said, "So what is 20 Euros, next to an experience of a lifetime?" I decided to put it on Black and there were cheers as it fell on 28 and I won my money back. "You *are* lucky, darling," the woman insisted. "What's your favourite number?" I told her it was 17 and she just gave me the eye, I knew exactly what she meant.

I gave my chips to the croupier and everyone cheered and clapped. I could start to see how people get so into gambling. I think having all those people watching made a big difference, I've never been tempted to bet on horses or whatever, but it was such a buzz having an audience, usually I'm behind the camera, trying to be as anonymous as possible. I think I liked being the centre of attention, yet without anyone knowing or caring who I was.

I squeezed her hand again as the wheel started spinning. It fell nowhere near, and the croupier raked in more of my money. I tried another €20 on Red and it fell on Black – I'd lost fifty quid, or thereabouts. "I guess I'm not so lucky after all," I said to the woman, and got up to return my chips at the counter. As I got €50 back, the woman told me not to leave. I said it had been an *experience*, but I was done. I put on my cardigan and made for the exit. She followed me through the foyer, grabbing my arm and turning me around as I got to the door. "You *are* lucky," she said, and kissed me on the lips.

She asked me what my name was, and I don't know why but I told her *Monica*. "Come, Monica," she said as she took my hand and we ran past the fountain around the back of the casino, past the busts of Berlioz and Massenet. We sat under the one of Diaghilev and stared into each other's eyes. I could hear the sea in the background but it felt so calm, we kissed there and then she said she'd show me the city. She led me to the Plage du Larvotto – it was strangely quiet, I had no idea what time it was but it was dark, and the waves must've drowned us out as we found a little alcove and silently made out.

Then the fantasy broke. I said we couldn't go back to mine, as I was staying at a friends. (I couldn't bear to tell her about the bunk bed.) She kissed me again, took off her gloves and put them in her bag, then placed her hand on my thigh. Her skin felt so soft, so good, and there were just the tiniest gusts of wind. Unlike at the casino, there was no-one watching and I prayed that no-one would hear us. I realised, just for a second, that it was my first time with someone since we last spent a night together; one of those horrendous nights in December 2019 when I knew we were doomed; before I went out alone the next day, somewhere totally unglamorous, to have more doors slammed in my face. Now, one was opening, to where I didn't know. I whispered in her ear if we could go back to hers.

"I think my husband would like that," she said, and my heart broke again. I wished I'd not got so carried away and asked her earlier. Perhaps she – *Lou*, she said her name was – did this all the time and was used to not disclosing this information. Or more likely, she did, and they had some wild threesomes, but I wasn't in the mood and suddenly, didn't want to stay at this strange, too-perfect beach. I kissed her on the lips, turned and walked back up the hill without a word. Nobody spoke to me as I got back to the flat, took off my shoes, stripped off my red and white dress, and climbed back into my bunk.

*Hôtel de Paris*

*Café de Paris*

**From:** sergeant-rock@gmail.com
**To:** robinsonrj191@gmail.com
**Date:** 25 April 2022, 01:48
**Subject:** (no subject)

I got back to Gatwick Airport, took my phone off flight mode and your email came straight up. If that's what you think is best, then this will be the last time I write to you.

I was never trying to find "happiness" in Monaco. What did I ever say or do to make you think I was? I remember speaking with a friend years ago and they told me the likes of us "weren't put on this earth to be happy". We talked long into the night about how it made more sense to look for contentment. But having had my hopes raised and then ruined with you these last few years, I can't put stock in that either. For the most part, since lockdown, I've just been trying to do things I enjoy, as much as we've been allowed and as much as I feel up to it. I'll come back to politics later – if there's ever anything worth coming back for.

I don't know *what* I was looking for in Monaco tbh. I thought it might be interesting to see how people I've always hated actually live - if they were who I thought they were, and just for a few days, how I might position myself within that ... or be positioned ... or become someone else. I'm telling people I went there for work, which is true, but I *chose* Monaco, and then pitched something to Chris. And now I've just written to tell him I haven't really got anything for the assignment, and I expect he'll just not pay me and think twice about commissioning me again, but do you know what? I'm glad I went. I could probably have told you before I did (and you definitely would have) that the place is a strange mirage, a nation-as-confidence-trick, and that the woman I met was a fantasy – the kind you'd make up if you were trying to make your life sound more exciting. (And the kind who keeps coming up on the apps, with her equally implausible male partner, who rarely ever PM but who I ignore when they do …) But so what? It was a lot weirder than I expected, not always in a bad way, and it made me wish we could all live surrounded by art and beautiful gardens without all these things being gated away like they are at home.

It's strange, and sad, being back in London. I got the train through those dismal Tory suburbs where I grew up – I hate having to see Redhill again almost every time I go away, and the journey home through them always lasts forever – thinking about having to deal with my housemates again, let alone having another of those long conversations with mum where she finds some reason to stop herself meeting people and picking herself up. You remember how we'd stop for homeless people in Dalston, sitting down for a chat and then getting up, looking south and seeing all those towers in Bishopsgate, a new one with some stupid cloying name every week, designed to make you feel the impossibility of socialism conquering it all? It's even worse now, and every time I come back from somewhere else, I feel the cold and wet of that December and the unbearable misery of that January. I wish this country could just be as honest – the reason we don't have banlieues or Beausoleil is because they're at the heart of the city.

Anyway, I'm listening to Léo Ferré as I write this, Soph is away so I've turned it up a bit, but I should probably go to bed. Of course I still wonder where you are, what you're doing, and who you're with. But you're right, it's better I don't know, that you don't tell me, and that I do the same. To put it another way: *We shall not see each other ever.*

TOOTHGRINDER PRESS

**'Monaco'**
**Juliet Jacques**
**TG0017**

First edition | Published 2023
100% recycled & unbleached paper
Printed in the UK

Design by William Francis Green
Edited by Edward Julian Green
Photography by Juliet Jacques

toothgrinderpress.com
toothgrinderuk@gmail.com
@toothgrinderpress

No part of this publication may be reproduced, stored in a retrieval system or transmitted in any form by any means without prior permission in writing of the appropriate individual author or artist, nor be otherwise circulated in any form of binding or cover other than in which it is published and without a similar condition including this condition being imposed on the subsequent purchaser.

Copyright © Juliet Jacques
ISBN: 978 1 80068 908 4